GOTHIC HIGH

by the same author

Graffiti, 1954
Less Is More, 1978

GOTHIC HIGH

GOLDIAN VANDENBROECK

LINDISFARNE PRESS

COVER: Bourges Cathedral
Photograph: Serge Moulinier

Published by the Lindisfarne Press
RR 4, Box 94A-1
Hudson, New York 12534

Library of Congress Cataloging-in-Publication Data is
available upon request.

ISBN: 0-940262-52-5

Graphic Consultant: Paul Parpard

CONTENTS

for
AVB
AOR
& JF

Focussing on the French Gothic cathedrals, Goldian VandenBroeck's sonnets draw upon specific factual data of execution as well as outcome. But what is special about these poems is their imaginative insights, their vibrant images and felicitous turns of phrase, their rich nuggets of allusion culled from as far back as antiquity. They reveal the vivid panoply of energy and innovation, of praise and aspiration, of wonder, which were embodied in these astonishing triumphs of man's spirit. And in the process, we are conjured into sharing and being deeply moved by the vision which originally motivated the builders' many-splendored creations.

John Fitchen

The arch upon the square creates the vault,
the arch upon the circle sires the dome;
upon the pointed arch's somersault
springs up this steep mediæval honeycomb
and with the arch the buttress comes alive
and flies straight sideways to the nave's vast prayer
—God's the honey of this Gothic hive,
forever crystallizing in mid air
—infinitely proportioned to true measure,
transparently projected up the sky,
dissolving in its windows' tinctured treasure,
stone upon stone, stands numberless hands high,
    tall walls to stained glass masterfully thinned
    transcending time's iconoclastic wind

Far, far above the world of the parvis
where springing arches interpenetrate,
huge nave vaults loft the stellar apogee
these sweeping columns subtly culminate
—as if the Architect who plotted Earth
charged: *Let there be a great cathedral here,*
the ogive's revolutionary birth
upholds new heights where the buttresses rear;
unswervingly deploying their invention
by siphoning fierce pressures off the walls,
gravitating toward the sun's ascension
through the glass glory of these quarried halls;
    this stone-shaped space of powered weightlessness
    surging vertically diaphanous

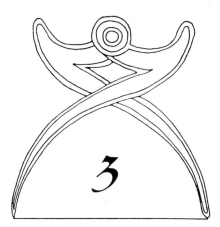

The first of the stones lays the foundation,
the cube on which the whole cathedral stands,
the cornerstone embodying creation
of Earth and its cathedral-building hands:
rays of ribs diverge in all directions
like jets of water from an icy fount,
merging back into their own reflections
across the alpine nave's mediæval mount
whose seamless joints deceive the dazzled eye
to think the building but a single stone
from caverns of the crypt that underlie
to the cloud-shrouded spire's audacious cone,
    with all its reverent concinnity
      tapering off into infinity

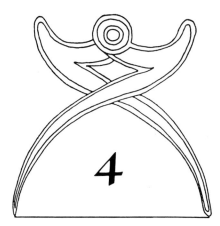

The cornerstone, huge cubic hieroglyph
from which the sacred structure radiates
foursquare —the very kernel of the myth
the stretching of the base cord orchestrates—
anchors the rock the whole cathedral flies
free of its earth-bound body's massive weight,
and strongly vaulting its interior skies,
centers reverence in its deepest state
—an architectural legerdemain
transposing stones into a lucid text
cathedralizing spaces arches span
with cantilevered musculature flexed,
  each stone conforming to an iron law
   in temples that still make men freeze with awe

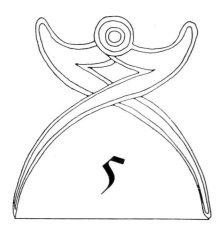

Suddenly appears the steep façade,
sheer looming cliff of populated walls
—surprisingly as face to face with God—
still flushed with sunset as the evening falls;
half hard mirage, half spiritual fort,
long poised to rocket off the parvis floor
with its majestic Pilot holding court
above the sculpture of the royal door,
before a chorus carved of rapt immortals,
flat, elongated figures, chaste and fresh,
around the panoply of western portals
in pulsating tableaux of fine stone flesh:
    across the fateful square of the parvis,
    all's *cathedral* as far as eyes can see

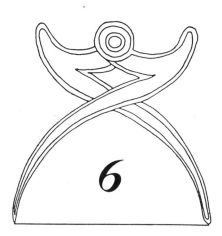

Pull the heavy leather door and enter
this steeply rising world of soundless stone;
lingering in the narthex, surrender
to the cathedral's ethereal zone
and entering again, time after time,
discover the persistence of the spell
compelling the reflective eye to climb
the superstructure of this Gothic shell;
no matter how familiar be the sight
of solid columns flying off the ground
or glinting windows streaming deep-dyed light,
these mysteries unfailingly astound,
    meticulously charted and designed
      to scale the Himalayas of the mind

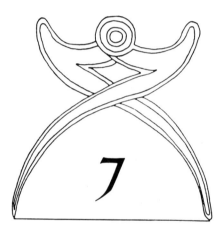

Paradise, surprisingly mediæval,
a separate world occulted bulwarks shore
—immortal forest, inwardly primeval,
awaits behind the frontier of the door
and lifts us swiftly far beyond our lives,
above ourselves, up to exalted realms
where the vaulting's meridian arrives
on piers that grow to dwarf enormous elms;
polished columns solidly implanted
branch out to rib each nave bay's taut stone cell:
quarriesful of sculpture stand enchanted,
composing an unearthly citadel,
    the peaked ogive's miraculous device
    begetting replicas of paradise

8

"Ars sine Scientia nihil est."
Jean Mignot
Milan, 1390

Slowly into being came the arch
that points to heaven, stone arms raised in prayer;
swift ranks of flaring arcs in upward march
as if constructed on a taunting dare,
culminate in solemn colonnades
of columns leafed into the rib vault's thrust
whose fierce expansion silently parades
this spiritual fabrick culled from earthen crust;
great chords of frozen music rise   sky   high
in contrapuntal buttresses' embrace,
stone sweep of rhythmic galley oars reply
to tense trajectories of inner space,
     proving Art is nothing without Science
     to underpin this levitating silence

9

Akimbo, head flung back in fascination
—the visitor's riveting reflex,
immemorial stance of exaltation,
sure signature of temple architects:
behold the climax of the crystal cliffs
immuring heaven in this stone abode
—carved symbolique of Gothic megaliths
the pointed arches visibly decode—
and follow the geometrizing hand
that improvised the thrusts the tall walls pose,
unleashing pressures buttresses withstand
to orb the glory of the stained-glass rose
    so that we might unknowingly exalt
    old ratios still holding up the vault

LINDISFARNE PRESS publishes works of new science, psychology, religion, literature, metaphysics, and spirituality.

If you would like to be on our mailing list and receive a catalog, please fill out and return this card.

Name _____

Street _____

City _____

State _____

Zip

Thank You

LINDISFARNE PRESS
RR 4, BOX 94 A1
HUDSON, NEW YORK 12534-9420

Beneath the nave's far overarched embower,
the aisle's receding vista richly dawns
where high-pitched arcades of the choir empower
transparent walls the pointed archway spawns;
all trace of buttressing concealed from sight
by stained glass steeping in its metals' fire,
suspended to illuminate the height
of lofty walls assembling ever higher,
—straight up the structure's cloistered universe—
pierced through and through by rays of ancient sun
as facets of the magic glass disperse
their ultraviolet phenomenon,
    indelibly, unerringly highflown
    by deft manipulation of the stone

No form so pleases looking as the arch
refined to implement the Gothic dream,
designed to overreach the mountain larch
—no longer two thick uprights and a beam—
it opens onto heaven's beckoning
with curvature of tapering voussoirs
wedged in with geometric reckoning
concisely calibrated as guitars,
so tightly tuned if struck each would expound
the whole cathedral in its every part,
each passageway uplifted to compound
the pointed arch's scientific art,
　　　initiating this stone tour de force:
　　　　space without enclosure, light without source

12

Despite ourselves, the huge vault lifts our gaze,
captured by the architect's intention:
up to the highest contemplation raise
perpendicularity's invention;
the crown thrust operating through the arch
resolves the mystery of spanning space
as the slow-setting mortar's hardy starch
steels the boldly reeling vault without a trace,
still brandishing an equilibrium
of stone ribs spreading outward like a fan
in answer to an ancient conundrum
opposing wingèd gods and anchored man,
    baring to the gazer's contemplation
    spirit's architecturalization

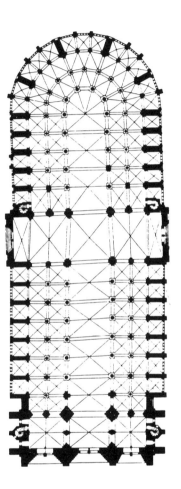

Mosaics of the aisle now pave the moss
that led into this sacramental grove
whose Druid hearth beneath the altar's cross
still shows old testimonials to Jove;
entirely to house the ancient glade
inside the vast cathedral's branching room
—stone foliage of faces in the shade
of stone trees bursting into chiseled bloom—
and roof the forest over with a nave
enveloping the dolmen's holy spell,
primordial temple of the cave
within the bell-jar of this Gothic dell,
    overtones of Rome and Greece and Egypt
    resounding through the new cathedral's crypt

The power of antiquity prevails
and vibrates down the ages through these stones,
growing where the old cathedral dovetails
the sky, and holds the reminiscent bones
of centuries asleep in alabaster,
below, amid the crypt's cyclopean blocks,
beneath the nameless chisel of a master
binding the time antiquity still clocks:
Christ's triumphal arches in procession
along the nave aisle's meditating spine
conjugate in vertical expression
the lapidary verbs that vault the shrine
    in noble ratios of sacred style
      established by the temples of the Nile

Leafing back through history's fading pages,
this time-begrimed cathedral towers white,
diminishing perspective of the ages
finds it shimmering in the champagne light:
the architect who animates these stones
arrives at the construction, gloves in hand,
grandmaster of the theory practice hones,
cathedrals spring to life at his command:
"Cut thus," he indicates with compass prod,
perceiving the buttress latent in the rock,
"Here's where you cut for me —and build for God,"
and for the dense throngs of the ardent flock
    performing pilgrimage upon the maze
    this sole-smoothed, knee-worn pavement still displays

In rich profusion this cathedral's grown
on clustered columns, pier after pier;
hands slowly laying silent stone on stone
raised this tabernacle, tier upon tier;
an elegantly skeletal device
of joints too fine to pass a color through,
in measurements eternally precise
and in proportion gloriously true;
stone bones of its acutely arching lines
positioning the building's lean physique,
the radiant space within these confines
dictating revolutionized technique,
    for nerves and sinews of its frame laid bare
    show how the structure dovetails with the air

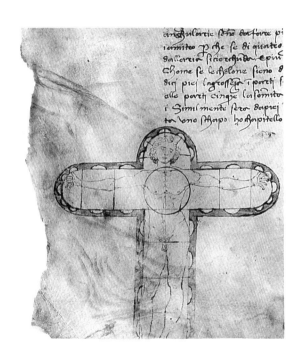

Springing from the ground in one stone voice,
the Word made stone with Gothic eloquence
to edify, aspire, and rejoice
in luminosity, life's radiance,
flooding the sanctuary with its rays
of *Lux continua,* sacred leaven
fermenting that sublime mediæval craze
to build the very scaffolding of heaven:
a sudden white of churches cloaked the land,
arising, as by some alchemic yeast,
where God the Architect, compass in hand,
plants Royal Man, spread-eagle, heading East,
    no longer crucified against the skies
    but towering in the shape of paradise

Of all the many mansions of thy god
—each architecturally spectacular
—Delphic as the pyramid's true tripod
and as ineffably oracular—
none knows more intimately to enthrall
than this cathedral's lapidary stance
that liberates the fortress of the wall
with buttresses leashed tight in rampant prance,
henceforth to frame the spaces in between
these braces with vast sheets of colored glass
whose iridescent spectrum's lustrous sheen
the rainbow's Roman arch cannot surpass,
 and here alone, at the heart of the choir,
 only descant rises any higher

Released from gravity's possessive clutch,
cathedrals spring—like Eve—from a rib, fullblown,
beneath the sculptors' metamorphic touch
tapping the pristine nature of the stone;
evoking to the surface of its form
the slow pulse of the mineral domain
the emblematic windows gently warm
and bathe in the cryptic tinctures of their stain;
wresting from rock the new cathedral's soul
a solid masonry will engineer
into a radiating aureole,
tiara of the chapel's hemisphere,
    blazing the nimbus of the curving apse
    with pyrotechnic flares the glass enwraps

This is what men once knew to do with light,
these stones stretched thin to let new colors through,
displaying famed glass-masters' brilliant sleight
in unimaginable red and blue;
the sanctuary's spiritual lumen
blindingly arriving from the East,
greeted here by choirs divinely human,
Gothic voices spiraling, priest to priest,
murmurously celebrating Latin
these arches supersonically resound
off centuries of stone worn smooth as satin,
manoeuvred to re-echo—and astound—
    resonating Logos, psalm by psalm,
    like incense permeating Notre Dame

Pure radiation of the window's rose,
translucent boon brought back from the Crusades
—ennobled glaziers, only, can compose
the reds and blues illuming these arcades;
curved and countercurving shells of chapels
proportioned in chromatic overtones,
carved lace tracing glass whose essence dapples
the chalky bare bones of these high-strung stones:
vast mandalas of ruby and sapphire
invisibly suspended from sheer height
reverberate the visionary choir,
for bright is that which brightly couples bright
    when through the jeweled mosaic of the glass
    great rays of palpitating sunlight pass

22

Bathed in its northern windows' indigo,
framed by the branching antlers of these trees,
the pale cathedral glistening in the snow
—the traffic-blackened statues of its frieze
swathed in the hoarfrost's phosphorescent veil—
looms like a Gothic glacier through the sleet,
imperviously weathering the gale
and the drifting chiaroscuro of the street;
now improvising vaults of thick-ribbed ice
inside the blizzard's chiseling barrage:
white icon of an arctic paradise
projecting the cathedral's cold mirage,
    donning the snow's phantasmagoric form,
    wild whirlwind architecture of the storm

Flawlessly ascending without falter,
already underground the towers start,
the vaulting starts its arching with the altar,
the new cathedral's subterranean heart
anchored in its venerable crypt
as deep as tall, like roots of soaring trees
(full many a bearded brother mason slipped,
a hero, from the scaffolding's trapeze);
weights, thrusts, and measures ritually planned
to float the whole cathedral in the light,
its deepest chasms vertically spanned,
pulsing rib cage of buttresses in flight,
    ascending skyward block by quarried block,
    strong as a sphinx hand-hewn from living rock

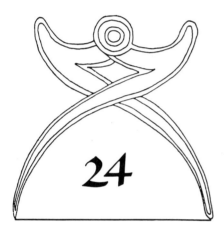

Long ago —when the cathedrals were white,
flinging their passion high against the sky,
articulating their fantastic height
to raise the heavy-lidded earthly eye—
the measured musing of the architect
calculating higher, thinner, tighter,
perfected curving groins that intersect
and arch an inscape pointed as a mitre
—spawning a breed of priestly steeplejacks:
sun floods in this crystalline arena
because of their devout highwire acts.
Though white cathedrals now wear dark patina,
    their exoskeletons of stained-glass skin
       still vanquish gravity's harsh discipline

These weightless stones transfigured by the hand
wielding the compass far above the quarry,
commemorate the vaulting mind that planned
the feat of setting story upon story:
in each of the four corners lies a stone
upon which two ribbed pointed arches tread,
for wise *Geometras* had always shown
that they would clearly crisscross overhead;
pitched in an unswerving state of tension
tuned by the artful master like a harp,
exulting in the daredevil invention
of the high-flying buttresses' escarp,
    taut bows holding volatile and aery
      the arches' and the rib vaults' thrust and parry

Diagonally intersecting in mid air,
the acrobatic nerves of the cross-ribbed vaults
still coolly launch their bracing network's flare
terrestrial attraction scarcely halts;
webbed ribs fanning out to spring through space,
meshing with the nave's immense dimension,
land perfectly with calculated grace
quickening their energetic tension;
gathering thrust along the groin vaults' ridges,
leap far to meet their structural respond,
spanning the transept's vast suspension bridges,
immaculately form a perfect bond
    because the agile arches never rest
    (Ars sine Scientia nihil est)

All overgrown where tree-trunk columns stood,
the ruined abbey sprawls into the grass
—ribs branching into this encroaching wood,
shattered tracery clasping missing glass;
smashed, mined, and pillaged for its building stock,
long pious aisles now open to the stars;
these prostrate statues turning back to rock
bear dynamite's raw vandalizing scars
—demolished, but the sacred space it housed
where reverential centuries once trod
still shudders where the plunderers caroused
and blew to bits its stones' indwelling god:
    its builders' vision taken to the grave,
    imagination vaults this butchered nave

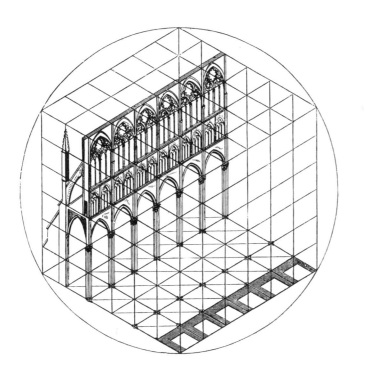

As crystals form along the unseen lines
that hold the sixfold snowflake in position,
the pointed arch implicitly defines
this cathedral's lacy apparition,
its spreading net of carved and polished nerves
of groined vaults that diagonally cleave,
becoming volumes, verticals, and curves
stemming from the sharpened peak of the ogive;
far overhead, stone cobwebs of the nave
in highest flights of masonry festoon
the necessary ways the vaults behave:
devoutly planned, hand-quarried and hand-hewn,
    in just proportion still stand tautly wrought
    for Art without Geometry is naught

Immensities of upward surging power
as in a lust of building ever higher
—beginning in the crypt to launch the tower
and dizzying ascendancy of spire—
ignited the desire for unknown height
based on antiquity's eternal fire,
perfected for the worship of the light
flooding the hemicycle of the choir:
the walls from their supporting toil released,
thick walls replaced by bright transparent skin
with espalier of buttresses increased
to let the windows' jeweled rays stream in:
    it falls not, realized in stone on rock,
      this Viking vessel berthed in a Gothic dock

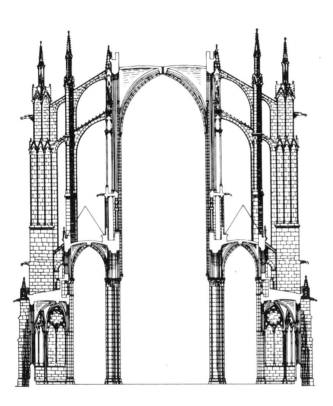

Sail past the sculptured sentries at the door
into the cathedral's steep-walled harbor,
navigate the narrows where columns soar
overhead, with visionary ardor;
fast propelled on the buttresses' galley
sculling the bulwark's timber, ashlar-oared,
across the keel of the vessel's valley,
over the archscape of the nave's stone fjord;
dock in the anchorage of its quarried hull
with pinnacles unfurling flying jibs
and soar with the effervescence of a gull
on the Gothic rig of its springing ribs,
    shored by the force of each enormous stave
    bracing the inverse shipyard of the nave

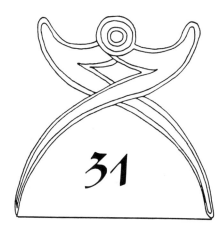

Fashioned by a race of building giants,
great clustered pillars ranged in silent file
demonstrate their sacerdotal science
along the quiet boulevard of the aisle;
slow cadence of the columns' promenade
accelerating overhead to surge
the elongated piers' swift escalade
toward which stone lines of upward thrust converge;
to raise the nave's celestial palisade
on stone drums culminating in carved space,
the master boldly flung his colonnade
to serve the superstructure as a brace
    whose arches imperceptibly convey
    the stress of pressures buttresses relay

Entirely constructed to enthrone
a visionary image magnified:
a mother and a child cajoled from stone
—the Logos-bearing torch personified;
light wafting through the structure like perfume
to shape a fragrant chamber for a queen,
vast castle of the nave's celestial room
reflected in its own stones' ivory sheen;
immense reliquary of stained-glass jewels
glittering in metaphysic splendor
as if its artists used no human tools
on stone become miraculously tender,
    crystallizing in a virgin's palace
      raised up by its village like a chalice

Wood-workers, masons, glaziers: craftsmen all,
down to the lowly bearer of the hod,
a race of builders glorifying Gaul
as high as hands can reach, to dovetail God;
roving brotherhood of the artifex:
quarryman, carpenter, sculptor, and the smith,
long lineage of dauntless architects
all intent on the cathedral's monolith;
chisels, mallets, axes, compass, augers,
lagging, windlass, templates, hurdles, cerce;
apprentice, journeyman; wheelwrights and loggers;
above all, an inexhaustible purse,
    for gold was the mortar of this giant grail,
    holding the stones that clasp its stained-glass veil

Sheathed in space, a mighty stained-glass cage
free of its own construction's vast expanse
—rising until the eye cannot engage
its climbing volumes in a single glance—
lifts the exclusive beauty of this place
up through its stones' hermetic firmament:
the solid scaffolding of Gothic space
renders this levitation permanent—
arching across the transept's precipice
the sacrosanct proportions of the nave,
refining with intrepid artifice
the stronghold of its heavenly enclave,
    the battle over gravity well won
      in the immortal unction of the sun

Kaleidoscopic nimbus of the rose,
focus of its halo's glowing petals,
this cathedral's scintillating windows
tinctured with the essence of pure metals,
like rare wine hold up red glass to the light
—a salamandrine red of unknown source
that ranks its glazing innovator knight
and guardian of the enigmatic force
producing blues of somber indigo—
igniting the cathedral's sacred spark,
lingering long past sunset's afterglow
in waning rays that blaze the holy dark,
    articulated seamlessly to fuse
    windows of solar reds and lunar blues

Glass cathedrals, spacious aviaries
capturing the flight of buttressed towers
hovering above the sanctuaries'
seasonless garden of stained-glass flowers,
unimaginable incandescence
the dissolution of the walls displays,
stone holy of holies' flowing essence
ecstatic verticality conveys
in waves of fluttering buttresses aligned
to brace the curvature of mammoth strands
the geometric conduct of the mind
arches, and polyphonically commands
    up to the zenith where these ogives meet,
    unswervingly performing their stone feat

Now towering alone above the town,
the centering frames—its armature—all gone,
the scaffolding completely taken down,
the folding wedges breathlessly withdrawn,
the new cathedral standing on its own
solidifies around its spark divine
and animates Creation, stone by stone,
through templates of celestial design;
framing heaven plumb with spirit level
to posit arches high above the ground,
mounting glass walls in its framework's bezel
with forces catapulted to rebound,
    unfolding the umbrellas of the vault
    to rise above the rooftops, white as salt

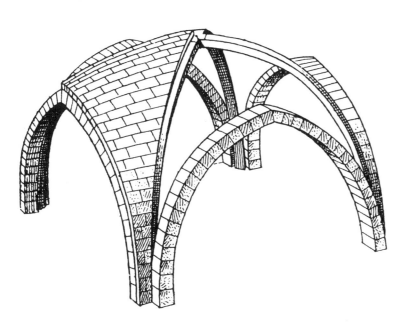

Two arches interlocking spawn the vault
and pitch its floating bulk athwart the nave,
taking the heights of heaven by assault
up parapets its slim ribs swiftly brave;
past galleries of sheer clerestory tiers,
through rooted shafts of soaring bundled sheaves;
the Gothic sap still rising up these piers
bends the vaults toward the curve of their ogives,
each fastened with a single giant bolt
tethering the arch that will not slumber,
quickening to spire from archivolt
the mysterious presence of number,
    arched high upon its stones' eternity
     in towering equipoise of symmetry

Curving imperceptibly to tether
the billowing tents of the starry naves,
far-flung arches polarize together,
fast in a circuitry of stone bouquets;
pitching the cathedral in suspension
with web vaults pinioned by their lofty keys,
new altitudes of ogival invention
honing the camber of their symmetries;
exercising every stone's resilience
throughout the arches' elasticity
to stretch the stained-glass windows' vivid brilliance
upon the structure's taut plasticity,
    immuring space transparent colors play
      and overtones of plainchant ricochet

for Aor

The mystery of each morning's genesis
decants its fluid elemental light
into the choir's translucent edifice
faint rays of dawn's emblazonry ignite
so shadows now accentuate the structure
upon the very stones of which it grows,
showing the vaults' vertiginous conjuncture
as day crescendoes in the stained-glass rose;
oriented toward the morning's scission
dividing sunrise from the night's deep dye,
the glass enacts its heavenly transmission
somewhere between the window and the eye
    —look, juxtaposed shards of its red and blue
    fuse purple in the contemplating view

Stone upon stone, arising course on course,
mounting the cathedral's bold ascension,
the stone's dead weight now turned to active force
—every arch and strut at bowstring tension;
each clustered pier a vibrant, sonant mass
towering in gravity's defiance
that solid walls might be replaced by glass
where light and color marry their alliance:
the constant restlessness of upward flight
to the ultimate point of its ascendant
high overhead where springing ribs unite
leaves the structure airily resplendent,
    the stranglehold of gravity defied
    as if the stones had magnets set inside

The great wheel—hauled aloft by the windlass—
revolved by treading men within its drum
raises the tracery of the window's glass,
hoists the capitals of each huge column
to structure walls that let the sun flood in
the translucent mosaics of the bays
—glass tapestries stretched perilously thin
to catch each facet of its shifting rays:
against the day, the tracery spins stark
as blackest velvet tightly hemming gems
whose burning colors slanting through the dark
play on the slender nave piers' soaring stems,
    stone streams of forces rising from the floor,
    vanquishing gravity, endlessly soar

Builded so high it could not fail to fall
for having flown too closely to the sun,
the fiercely headstrong vaulting of the hall
by earth's magnetic jealousy undone;
the inbuilt hubris of its fatal flaw
remains to haunt the vestige of this site
and pay for flouting gravity's fixed law
with transcendental walls of stained-glass light:
stone's adamantine soul, transfigured here,
set free and daringly attenuated,
stretched up to spire the very aerosphere
the sharply pointed arch accentuated,
    but breaching summits all the gods tabooed
    collapsed its soaring folly's altitude

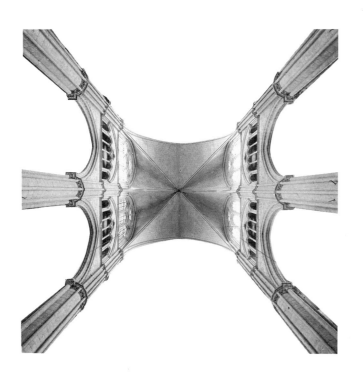

Improvisation on the antique theme
of building to the uttermost reaches,
arrived at this cathedral's bold extreme
of sheer ascent its very structure preaches;
rich variations on the art that spans
uninterrupted distances with stone;
vast stained-glass lightship God supremely mans,
steered by the spires the thundrous bells intone;
with all the nerve infinity excites,
towers architecturally bolder,
erecting the intoxicating heights
tilting back the head of the beholder;
    raised on its pointed arches' flexing brawn
    so high the eye feels deeply inward drawn

"Mayest thou, who hast built a new
dwelling for thyself through us,
cause us to be received in the
dwelling of Heaven . . ."
                    Abbot Suger, 1144

Vault altar roof spire scaffold timber nave,
gable crocket pinnacle tympanum,
flèche rib bay buttress tower architrave,
statue pillar pier arch aisle organum ;
windlass stained-glass voussoir keystone trefoil,
column chapel transept tracery walls,
ogive cloister corbel portal gargoyle,
clerestory lantern spandrel crown strut stalls;
porch belfry steeple parvis colonnade,
capital crypt mosaic labyrinth,
ambulatory mortar balustrade,
apse façade triforium lintel plinth,
    template gantry lagging ashlar gilding,
    hauling hewing carving hoisting: building

Once the glacier's sculpting tongues receded,
cathedrals dormant in the valleys' rock
revealed themselves to be the quarries needed
for tall vaults time and space would interlock:
Between the stones the mortar's pungent lime
and living water slowly coalesce
the heights of this celestial paradigm
whose chiseled pulse of stress and counterstress
produces lucent rooms so grandiose
to cube their huge proportions from these rocks
extrapolates from ancient ratios
techniques completely new, unorthodox
    —revolutionarily mediæval—
     to steel the pointed arch's steep cathedral

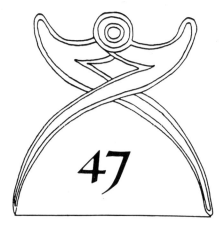

From those old quarries came this prized freestone
so easily chiseled without splitting,
ideal for the large and heavy keystone
at the crucial juncture of its fitting
high at the crown where all vault ribs unite
as floatingly as if there were no vault
above the fiery essence of the light
mingling stained-glass crimson and cobalt
to captivate the scrutinizing gaze
absorbed in slow prismatic vertigo
where filmy colors on the structure graze
fluorescent rays of limpid indigo:
    accomplishing the whole cathedral's goal,
    a total huge impression fills the soul

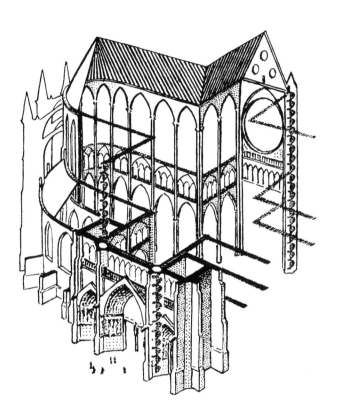

Arising ever higher from the ground,
the live cathedral's Gothic stratosphere
soars on its sharpened arches' upward bound
across the canyons valiant ogives clear,
and sheathes the open sky with stained-glass walls
contrived to compass slanting spokes of sun
from vaulted peaks the pointed arch installs
to forge an otherworldly eidolon;
divine perspective launched through time and space
down the wide aisle to the choir of its heart,
the spine of this transparent carapace
—spurred by the mobile power of its art,
     breaks from the sway of earth's magnetic sod
     and catapults directly into God

49

Stupendous silhouette against the clouds
above the landscape, awesomely aloof
from crypt of ancestry in chiseled shrouds
to captive gargoyles brooding on the roof;
magnetizing from its vibrant altar
in upward aim the goal of heaven drives:
a heaven stratified of purest ashlar
crowning the town with its lodestar of lives,
defining vertical immensities
enveloping the vessel of this ark
whose tinted windows' steeped intensities
disseminate light's quintessential spark,
    seat of the glass cathedral's solar throne
    fixed in the sacred constancy of stone

No longer stone but light, the walls dissolve
and disappear in function of the glass
whose glazed mosaic colorings revolve,
mysteriously tinctured in the mass;
the walls dissolve, no longer stone but light
the chiseled lace of tracery encloses
where centuries of dawning days ignite
the molten vortex of the glowing roses,
now barely deepening as evening's calm
suffuses the cathedral's cosmic room,
when twilight fires each window's oriflamme
and stained-glass embers coruscate the gloom
    as through the dim dusk of the nave's ravine
    their burning rubies turn ultramarine

Farther up, and farther yet the vision
wanders over tower, arch, and spire
meticulously flaunting their precision
above the stained-glass curtains of the choir
where the lithe ligature of ribs upholds
the grid of its supporting filigree
to drape stone vaults in neatly pleated folds
approaching the cathedral's apogee;
the thick lead sheets of its empyreal roof
where contemplative gargoyles coldly nest,
accentuate the structure's warp and woof
as it nears the crescendo of its crest,
    the whole cathedral heaven's divining rod
    —a single feather on the breath of God

ACKNOWLEDGMENTS

COVER: Bourges cathedral. One of the square six-part bays of the nave with its piers and transverse rib vaulting. Photograph: Serge Moulinier. In François Cali's *L'Ordre ogival: Essai sur l'architecture gothique*. Paris 1963.

TITLE PAGE: Stone labyrinth (40 ft. diam.) inlaid in the nave pavement of Chartres cathedral.

INTRODUCTION: John Fitchen III (1905–1990) was Professor of Fine Arts at Colgate University. One of the world's foremost authorities in the field of Gothic architecture, he was the author of *The Construction of Gothic Cathedrals: A Study of Medieval Vault Erection*, Oxford 1961 and *Building Construction Before Mechanization*, Cambridge 1986. Other works include *The New World Dutch Barn*, Syracuse 1968 and the now-classic article "Comment on the Function of the Upper Flying Buttress in French Architecture," *Gazette des Beaux-Arts*, 1955.

PAGINATION ORNAMENT: a proportion compass, a detail from the 13th century tombstone of Hugues Libergier, the architect of Saint-Nicaise of Reims, now in Reims cathedral. Symbol of a master builder, this type of compass is manipulated by working the two crossed legs from a common pivot. The High Middle Ages defined and practiced architecture as applied geometry.

1 The idealized Gothic cathedral as envisaged by Eugène Viollet-le-Duc in his *Dictionnaire raisonné de l'architecture française du XIe au XVIe siècle*. Paris 1858-1868. Viollet-le-Duc (1814-1879) was the dedicated restorer of the Sainte-Chapelle, Notre-Dame de Paris, the abbey church of Saint-Denis, the cathedral of Amiens and other mediaeval buildings.

2 God as Geometer-Architect of the Universe, using a master-builder's compass to create the world. Miniature from a 13th c. French Old Testament. Austrian National Library, Vienna. Cod. 2554, fol. 1v. "When he prepared the heavens, I was there: when he set a compass upon the face of the depth:" Proverbs 8:27 might have served to inspire the mediaeval architect who, in practicing the solid geometry of space, could come closest to imitating the work of his divine master.

3 Drawing by Viollet-le-Duc after a stained-glass window in Chartres donated by the cathedral stone-masons.

4 Study by Rodin from his *Cathédrales de France*. Paris 1914.

5 Bird's-Eye View of Paris: (detail) Notre-Dame and its parvis. From Matthieu Mérian's *Paris: Vol-d'Oiseau* map, 1615.

6 Chartres. Nave with labyrinth. In M.J. Bulteau's *Monographie de la Cathédrale de Chartres*, 1892.

7 "The Gothic Hut," built by Sir James Hall, author of *Essays on the Origins, History, and Principles of Gothic Architecture*. London 1813.

8 Paris: Notre-Dame. Aerial photo: Editions Chantal, Paris. *"Ars sine scientia nihil est,"*

that is to say, "skill without knowledge of geometry is worthless."

9 Bourges. Drawing: Dehio-Bezold, *Kirchliche Baukunst des Abendlandes.* Stuttgart 1892.

10 Building the Tower of Babel. Miniature from a 15th c. Flemish Book of Hours. British Library, London. MS. Add. 35313, fol. 34r.

11 Bury (Oise). Nave vaulting in village church, 1225. From *Development and Character of Gothic Architecture* by Charles H. Moore. New York 1904.

12 Toulouse, Eglise des Jacobins. "The Palm Tree." Brick apse vault resting on stone column 22 m. high and 1 m. 60 in diam., c. 1285. Photograph: Jean Dieuzaide. The "Preachers" church, opened wide by central pillars, was designed to accommodate huge audiences.

13 Paris: Notre-Dame. Ground plan after M. Aubert in *L'Architecture réligieuse en France à l'époque gothique* by R. de Lasteyrie. Paris 1926. Proof of the ancientry of Notre-Dame's site as a palimpsest of shrines came in 1711 when workmen repairing the choir unearthed four stone altars (now in the Cluny museum). One bears the name of Emperor Tiberius who reigned during Christ's lifetime. Thus the earliest date that can be associated with the Cathedral may be that of the Crucifixion! Caesar himself gave Roman names to the Druid gods he saw here in 53 B.C. (see A. Temko's *Notre-Dame*, 1952.)

14 "Elevation of the Vault." Drawing by A. Derderian in *The Horizon Book of Great Cathedrals.* New York 1968.

15 Drawing by Viollet-le-Duc on the title page of his *Dictionnaire. "Par ci me le taille"* : the famous words survive in a sermon delivered by Nicolas de Biard in 1261.

16 Construction site. From a 14th c. French miniature, *Les Grandes chroniques de Saint-Denis.* Bibliothèque Municipale, Toulouse. Photo: Studio Yan.

17 Ground plan of a church corresponding to the proportions of the human figure by Francesco di Giorgio, 15th c., parchment. Biblioteca Laurenziana, Florence.MS.Ashb. 361, c10.

18 Gothic construction system illustrating principles of isolated supports and buttressing. From *The History of Architecture* by A.D.F. Hamlin. New York 1915.

19 Paris: Saint-Germain-des-Prés. Exploded drawing by August Choisy in his *Histoire de l'architecture.* Paris 1899.

20 Paris: Notre-Dame. Elevation of the nave, drawing by Viollet-le-Duc, *op. cit.*

21 Chartres: Rose window in the west façade. From the *Album* of Villard de Honnecourt, c. 1225. Bibliothèque Nationale, Paris. MS. Fr. 19093. The most complete collection of mediaeval architectural drawings is the so-called "Album" or sketchbook of Villard de Honnecourt, a French master mason active between 1220 and 1235. This radial rose covers 650 square feet. *"Claret enim claris quod clare concopulatur"* ("For bright is that which is brightly coupled with the bright")—thc words are from Abbot Suger's inscription on the gilt bronze portals of the abbey church of Saint-Denis whose innovative reconstruction he

administered and consecrated in 1144, the first of the true Gothic stained-glass walled structures which permitted more light to pervade the entire building than ever before, thus setting the example for cathedrals to follow.

22 Amiens. Photograph by Wim Swann from his *Gothic Cathedral*. New York 1984.

23 Drawing by David Harris in Percy Watson's *Building the Medieval Cathedral*. Cambridge 1976.

24 Amiens, buttress and flying buttress, 13th c. *Encyclopédie de l'architecture et de la construction*, ed. P. Planat. Paris 1888.

25 Portrait of Eudes de Montreuil, Master-of-the-Works. Engraved from a 13th c. grave-slab, now destroyed. In Thevet's *Pourtraits et vie*, 1584. In *The Architect in History* by M.S. Briggs. Oxford 1927.
The Flemish poet Heinrich von Veldeke wrote the *Eneit*, his reworking of the *Eneas* in Thuringen dialect, in 1184: (In Paul Frankl's *The Gothic*. Princeton 1960)

"dâ lach in vier sinnen / vier steine wale gehouwen / die man gerne mochte skouwen/ dat seget man ons ongelogen. / drop stonden twêne swibogen / der wîse man Geometras /der des werkes meister was / he worchte sî met moete. / des konde er wale gerâmen,/ dâ si tesamene quâmenin / krûcewîs bovene."

"There lay in the four corners / four well-hewn stones / goodly to see. /This is told us truly./ On them stood two (rib) arches. / The wise man Geometras, / who was the master-of-the-work,/ he built them with care. /They were twenty feet high. / This he could well arrange /because they came together /crosswise above."

26 Amiens. The nave, looking east. Nineteenth c. drawing from *The Illustrated Dictionary of Architecture and Building* by Russell Sturgis. New York 1901.

27 Jumièges. Photographer unknown. Caisse nationale des monuments historiques et des sites. Considered to be the most evocative of French ruins, this 12th c. Normandy abbey was sold for its materials in 1789.

28 Amiens, the nave. From Joseph Gwilt's *Encyclopedia of Architecture*. London 1867.

29 The spires of Laon cathedral. Woodcut from Dusomerard. In *A History of Architecture in All Countries* by James Fergusson. London 1874.

30 Beauvais, cross-section. Drawing by Jean Duret in *Gothique*. Fribourg 1964.

31 Reims, flying buttresses of the apse. Drawing by Villard de Honnecourt. *op. cit.*

32 Amiens. Photograph: Courtesy of the Courtauld Institute of Art, London.

33 Hod carrier, masons, and stonecutter at work. *Grandes Chroniques de France*, miniature c. 1379. Bibliothèque Nationale, Paris.

34 "High-level Hung Scaffolding: Pier-Girdling Gantry Scheme." Drawing by John Fitchen from his *Construction of Gothic Cathedrals*. Oxford 1961. Reproduced by kind permission of the author.

35 Paris: Notre-Dame. Rose window in the north transept. Drawing by Painton Cowen in *Rose Windows*. San Francisco 1979.

Sometimes called "The Alchemists' Rose," this is considered to be "the supreme example of a rose window built up from a lattice of invisible geometry. [It] shows how the geometry creates and defines each concentric layer in a logical progression. The starting point is the centre of any one of the thirty-two outermost lights. By joining it to another, eight windows away, and continuing the process, an endless line is generated that takes in all of these outer lights. At the same time it creates a series of tangents to a circle which contains the centres of the next layer of thirty-two medallions. A similar operation repeated on this new layer —but this time by joining every eleventh window— creates two interlocking sixteen-pointed stars; and these in turn define the centres of each of the sixteen central windows containing the prophets. From these centres four interlocking squares can be drawn, which in turn tangentially produce the heavy red and gold halo around the Virgin and Child at the centre. Finally a sixteen-pointed star from this circle creates the opening for the central lights and the size of the openings that form the border of this central rosette. Thus the geometry relates every part to every other part and the totality to the point of focus—the centre."

36   Le Mans, the apse. From Ed. Corroyer, *L'Architecture gothique.* Paris 1891.

37   Coutances. In Furgusson, *op cit.*

38   Quadripartite web vault. In K.H. Clasen, *Die Gotische Baukunst.* Potsdam 1930.

39   Amiens. Vault system and the counter-buttressing of thrusts by the exterior buttresses. Drawing: Viollet-le-Duc, *op. cit.*

40   Amiens. The choir looking east. Etching by R. Garland. In *French Cathedrals* by Benjamin Winkles. London 1837.

41   "D'après un manuscrit de la librarie des fils du roi Jean." Thus reads the caption on this image in Planat, *op. cit.* Evidently a sketch for or from Jean Fouquet's 15th c. miniature, "Building the Tower of Babel."

42   Building scene with treadwheel. Miniature from a 13th c. Old Testament, French. By special permission of The Pierpont Morgan Library, New York. Drawing after MS. 638. f. 3r. detail. Stones, prepared by two men below, are lifted up by a windlass powered by a great wheel. A hod carrier is bearing mortar up the ladder.

43   Beauvais. Etching by H. Garland in Winkles, *op.cit.* (Internal height 157½ feet and the central span about 51 ft. wide.) The aspiration of the Gothic here reached its apogee, although Beauvais is only half a cathedral, being entirely without a nave. "Construction began in 1247. The choir was completed in 1272. Owing to the excessive frailty of the supports and the buttressing system, the vaults collapsed in 1284." (dates: H. Focillon) In the course of rebuilding, the transepts were begun. Between 1564 and 1569, before the nave was far advanced, a huge stone tower about 500' high was erected over the crossing. This collapsed in 1573, and no further construction ensued after repairing the damage. The tower was not rebuilt; the transepts with their rose windows survive and this truncated vestige is all that remains today. "Beauvais," wrote the 19th c.

novelist J.K. Huysmans, "is a melancholy fragment, having no more than a head and arms flung out in despair."

44   Bourges. Photograph by Serge Moulinier. Courtesy of the photographer.

45   "Girart de Roussillon and his wife, Berthe, Endow Twelve Monasteries in Honor of the Twelve Apostles." French miniature, 1447. Austrian National Library, Vienna. Cod. 2549, fol. 164r.

46   Construction of the Schoenau Monastery (near Heidelberg). Sixteenth c. drawing from frescoes supposed to have existed there. Nuremberg Germanisches Nationalmuseum, Kapsel 1532, H2196.

47   Strasbourg. In Furgusson, *op. cit.*

48   "Schematic Diagram of Circulation System: Vices and Passageways." Drawing by John Fitchen, *op. cit.* Reproduced by kind permission of the author.

49   "Le Penseur de Notre-Dame." Etching by John Taylor Arms in *Churches of France* by Dorothy N. Arms. New York 1929.

50   Traceries from Caen, Bayeux, Rouen, and Beauvais as drawn by John Ruskin in his "Lamp of Truth" in *The Seven Lamps of Architecture.* London 1849.

51   Paris: Notre-Dame. Unknown photographer. Sonnet inspired by "A Feather on the Breath of God," sequences and hymns by the Rhineland mystic, Abbess Hildegard of Bingen (1098–1179). Hyperion Records KA66039. London 1982.

FOLLOWING THE POEMS: An architect with a set square and a foreman's compass. Detail from a 13th c. miniature, *The Lives of the Offas.* British Library, London. MS. Cotton Nero D.I, fol. 23v.

GLOSSARY ILLUSTRATIONS:

The Architect. Viollet-le-Duc *op. cit.*

Builders. Drawing after a window in Chartres. In G.G. Coulton's *Medieval Faith and Symbolism.* Oxford 1928.

Construction of the Tower of Babel. Drawing after a 14th c. window in the church of Saint-Martin, Colmar. In P. du Colombier, *Les Chantiers des cathédrales.* Paris 1953.

Poitiers: cathedral choir stall: Unknown architect or workman, wood. Late 13th c. From P. du Colombier, *op. cit.*

"Green Man." Drawing of a carved foliage face by Villard de Honnecourt, *op. cit.*

Construction Site. Drawing after a window in Rouen cathedral. From G. Ritter, *Les vitreaux de la cathédrale de Rouen.* Cognac 1926

Masons at work. Detail from *The Book of Saint Albans*, 13th c. miniature. Courtesy of Trinity College, Dublin. TCD MS. 177.

Builders. Drawing by C. Kreutzberger after a 13th c. stained-glass window in Chartres cathedral. In Corroyer, *op. cit.*

BACK COVER: Hoisting devices. *Histoire Naturelle*, 13th c. Bibliothèque Municipale, Dijon.

DIAGRAMS

Ground Plan: Chartres, by R. Garland
In Winkles' *French Cathedrals*, 1836

Cross Section of Nave at Amiens :
Viollet-le-Duc, *Dictionnaire*, 1875

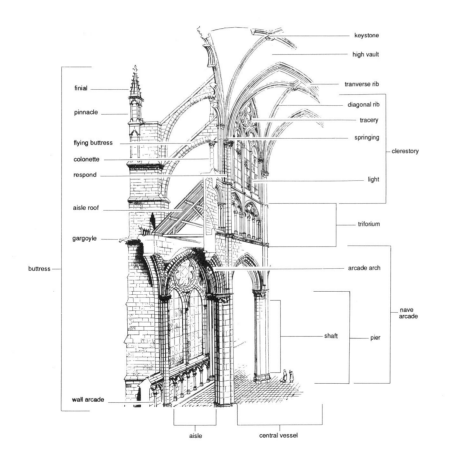

finial
pinnacle
flying buttress
colonette
respond
aisle roof
gargoyle
buttress
wall arcade

keystone
high vault
tranverse rib
diagonal rib
tracery
springing
clerestory
light
triforium
arcade arch
nave arcade
shaft
pier

aisle
central vessel

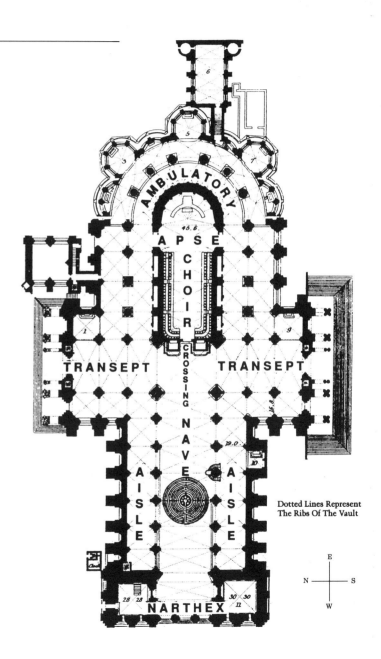

AMBULATORY
APSE
CHOIR
TRANSEPT
TRANSEPT
CROSSING
NAVE
AISLE
AISLE
NARTHEX

Dotted Lines Represent
The Ribs Of The Vault

GOTHIC GLOSSARY

AMBULATORY the curving aisle extension of the choir aisles for walking around the apse and giving access to altars and chapels

APSE the semi-circular eastern end of the cathedral; hemicycle or chevet

ARCADE a series of counter-thrusting arches and their supporting columns or piers

ARCH a curved self-supporting structure formed of wedge-shaped blocks (see Voussoirs) held together by mutual pressure which lock into position under gravity loads

ARCHITECT the definition of this term in the Middle Ages differed greatly from ours: it applied to a *magister operis*, "master-of-the-works," or master mason, who rose from the ranks in each specialty of the building procedures and who supervised the work in person together with the master carpenter in charge of the wooden parts: "A geometrician in the drafting of the plan, a mechanic in the assembling of the structure, a painter in the distribution of visual effects, and a sculptor in the treatment of masses. He assumes these different personalities in different degrees, according to the demands of his own spirit and to the state of the style in which he is working." (Henri Focillon)

ARCHITRAVE the horizontal lintel of a doorway or window, usually ornamented

ARCHIVOLT the inner curve of an arch or its wedge-shaped structural parts (see Voussoirs)

ASHLAR squared and hewn, dressed freestone ready for building; also, the masonry composed of such stones giving a pattern of horizontal and vertical joints

AUGER a carpenter's and joiner's tool for boring large holes

BAY one main compartment of vaulting defined externally by buttresses and internally by the transverse arches of ribbed vaults; also, a vertical unit of a nave wall

BUTTRESS a supporting mass of masonry attached to a wall as a solid anchor of the entire superstructure, serving to resist overturning and to receive and ground the lateral thrust of the arch or vault on its interior juncture; also, to receive wind loads

CAMBER a very slight rise or convex curve in an otherwise horizontal member, as in the crown of a pointed arch

CELL the curved infill between ribs and vault

CENTERING temporary construction of timber used to support masonry during the process of constructing arches, vaults, flying buttresses, etc. until the mortar dries

CERCE an extensible wooden device used to support the upper courses of stones in the construction of ribbed vaults

CHOIR the area extending from transept to apse reserved for the clergy; separated from the body of the cathedral by a screen or grille

CLERESTORY the upper stage of the nave wall above the aisles and triforium, pierced with a range of windows

COLONNADE a row of usually cylindrical columns set at regular intervals, usually supporting a roof or a series of arches

COLONNETTE a slender column not usually part of the primary structure

COLUMN a vertical structural member, supporting loads in compression (see Pier)

CORBEL a stone bracket projecting from the side of the nave wall and supporting a lintel, a statue, or the spring of an arch

COURSE in masonry, a horizontal line or row of stone blocks in a wall

CROCKET one of the small projecting spurs of foliate ornament on pinnacles

CROSSING the large central area defined by the central piers at the intersection of nave aisle, transept arms and choir; sometimes supporting a windowed tower called a lantern

CROWN the highest point of the curve of an arch or of a vault at which the diagonal ribs intersect

CROWN THRUST any true arch, being made up of wedge-shaped blocks, has a lateral thrust, and this action operates in all parts of the arch, not only at the spring and throughout the haunch, but also at the crown (JF)

CRUCIFORM cross-shaped in ground plan

CRYPT vaulted chamber or series of chambers beneath the sanctuary for tombs and relics, always the oldest part of a cathedral

DIAGONAL RIB the rib at the folded edge of a cross vault, diagonally crossing a bay of vaulting

DRUM one of the cylindrical blocks composing the shaft of a stone column

FABRICK the basic elements of the cathedral as a whole

FAÇADE the western front, facing the parvis, where the principal entrance doors are located

FINIAL the carved ornament at the apex of a pinnacle or spire

FLECHE a slender wooden spire rising from the roof over the point of the crossing, sometimes covered with lead, hallmark of French Gothic

FLYING BUTTRESS an arched masonry strut designed to transmit the vault thrusts to an outer support met and grounded by the buttress proper

FOURFOLD VAULT a quadripartite vault, the simplest form of cross vaulting in which two transverse arches, two diagonal ribs, and two wall ribs divide the vault into four compartments.

GALLERY a narrow space above an aisle with openings onto the main nave-body

GANTRY a framed structure raised on side supports so as to span a void, used to support centering or working platforms

GARGOYLE a waterspout projecting from a parapet, carved as an animal or human grotesque, designed to throw off the rain well away from the stone walls; also, the fantastic stone beings who inhabit the heights of Gothic cathedrals

GLAZING a collective term for the sheets or pieces of glass that fill a window opening, or the installation process thereof

GOTHIC this misnomer was originally applied in scorn by Italian architects of the Renaissance to a revolutionary mediaeval system of ogival architecture characterized by the pointed arch and ribbed vault produced by the combination of diagonal ribs with the groined vault. The epithet is inexact, the architectural style having no connection with the barbarous Goths

GREAT WHEEL a powerful device for raising weights, that works on the principle of the revolving squirrel cage

GROIN the projecting ridge, edge, or curved line formed by the supporting ribs of two intersecting vaults; also, the rib that covers this sharp edge

GROINED VAULT formed by the intersection of two barrel vaults at right angles

INSCAPE a term of multifarious meanings coined by the poet Gerard Manley Hopkins to communicate the individually distinctive inner nature of a form, as in "the strong and noble inscape of the pointed-arch." (See Ellen Eve Frank's *Literary Architecture* 1979)

JAMBS the vertical sides of a doorway or archway opening

KEYSTONE the central topmost wedge-shaped block or voussoir of an arch which locks the others in position. Until it is in place, no true arch action is incurred

LABYRINTH a Daedalian maze-like path inscribed or inlaid in the nave pavement, emblematic either of the difficulty or uncertainty of the Christian's progress through this world. Meant to excite religious devotion, it also represents a pilgrimage to the Holy Land, and mediaeval pilgrims re-enacted this, following its contours on their knees

LAGGING the temporary wooden forms on which the stones rest during the construction of a masonry vault until it is self-supporting

LINTEL a horizontal beam, usually decorated, forming the top of a door

NARTHEX the shallow entryway extending the width of the inner west front immediately behind the main portals

NAVE the main vessel or central area, beginning at the narthex and extending to the transept, devoted to the lay worshipper

OGIVE (ojeev) the French term used since the 13th century for the Gothic vault with its ribs and diagonally intersecting arches; a pointed arch

OGIVAL Gothic style

ORGANUM a mediaeval type of polyphony based on plainsong in which the voices are separated by an interval of a fourth, fifth, or octave

PARAPET low wall at the top of the cathedral projecting a roof gutter

PARVIS (parvee) the open square that fronts the cathedral; traditionally, a place of decision

PIER as distinct from a column, the compound pier grouped to support the aisle arches is composed of slender clustered colonnettes

PILLER an upright free-standing support

PINNACLE a small spire or turret atop a flying buttress to weigh it down

POINTED ARCH the apotheosis of Gothic architecture, composed of two arcs drawn from centers on the springing line

PORCH the more or less projecting doorways of a cathedral's principal portals

RADIATING CHAPELS chapels which project out from the ambulatory's radius

RESPOND a column or group of columns or a shaft attached to the nave wall, supporting a vault rib or arch

RIB a salient stone arch that supports a vault and divides it into compartments

RIBBED VAULT or RIB VAULT the cardinal and essential feature of Gothic vaulting, whereby a skeleton of arched ribs is first constructed and then covered by the thin web of the vault proper

RIDGE RIB the horizontal rib connecting the keystones along a series of vaults

ROSE WINDOW the circular stained-glass window set into geometrically patterned stone tracery, located near the top of the west wall and in each of the transept terminal walls

SANCTUARY the most sacred part of the cathedral, consisting of the four bays east of the crossing

SCAFFOLDING the temporary platforms supporting workmen and materials during construction

SPAN the spatial division across the building; the distance between the vault or arch supports

SPANDREL either of the triangular spaces between the exterior curve of an arch and a rectangular frame or mold enclosing it

SPRINGING the point or level from which the actual curve of an arch begins to curve upwards from its support

STALLS the carved wooden seats in the choir for the use of the clergy

STRESS the result in a structural component of the action of external forces upon it

STRUT a slender secondary structural member subject to longitudinal compressive forces

TEMPLATE a full-size wooden silhouette prepared for the masons to use in shaping the profile of a stone; any quantity of stones could thus be stenciled and cut

TENSION the stretching or degrees of stretching to which materials are strained by pulling forces or stresses

THRUST the sideways force or pressure of one part of a structure against another part, as of an arch against an abutment; the direction in which the weight of a vault pushes

TRACERY geometrically patterned stone framework clasping the glass of a window

TRANSEPT either of the two lateral arms of a cruciform cathedral

TREFOIL an ornament composed of three cusps in a circle

TRIFORIUM the wall area between the gallery and clerestory; a passage screened from the nave with an arcade of columns along its front; it covers the roof over the nave's side aisle

TYMPANUM the sculpted area above the lintel enclosed by the arch of a doorway

TRUE accurately fitted, exact, aligned; perpendicular or square to line or plane

VAULT a masonry ceiling of stone or brick based on the principle of the arch

VESSEL the main nave-body

VOUSSOIR a wedge-shaped stone used as a building block of an arch or vault

WEB the stone surface of a vault, seen as infilling between its ribs

WINDLASS a device for hoisting composed of a horizontal spindle with a long rope attached to it and supported at both ends. When it was turned, the rope would gradually be wound up around it

INDEX OF FIRST LINES